GEEZING ALONG AT 80:

Living, Loving and Laughing After Eighty

ANTHONY J. ANASTASI

L.R. Price Publications Ltd

GEEZING ALONG AT 80:
Living, Loving and Laughing After Eighty

Originally published by E-BookTime LLC, 2017.

This edition published by
L.R. Price Publications Ltd, 2019
27 Old Gloucester Street,
London, WC1N 3AX
www.lrpricepublications.com

Photographs courtesy of Anthony J. Anastasi
Copyright © Anthony J. Anastasi , 2018
Used under licence by
L.R. Price Publications Ltd.

The right of Anthony J. Anastasi to be identified as
author of this work has been asserted in accordance
with sections 77 and 78 of the Copyright, Designs and
Patents Act, 1988.

ISBN-13: 978-1916467927

ACKNOWLEDGMENTS

The Author would like to thank, wholeheartedly, the following contributors, who were instrumental in making this work possible: his dear literary wife, Jeanne, who remembered and rejoiced in so many of my stories; his original editor, Anne Mattison, who sculpted his verbiage so adroitly; his most helpful friend, Art Besner, whose comments on my work are superior to his writing; to Kimon Psira, for his creative, vibrant cover design on the original book; his family and friends, who have been so encouraging; and finally, thanks to his publisher L.R Price Publications even though they didn't like his (original) book title.

The Publisher would like to thank the following people: Len West, Susan Woodard, Matt Vidler and Russell Spencer for their hard work and support in making this book a reality.

DEDICATION

"Dedicated with endless love to my mother,
Virginia Spigone Anastasi."

GEEZING ALONG AT 80:

Living, Loving and Laughing After Eighty

ANTHONY J. ANASTASI

CONTENTS

14. "Is anybody up there going to help me?"

15. Making connections.

16. Daily routine.

17. Ahh, the old days.

18. The resume and the eulogy.

19. Extra points in heaven.

20. Keira, believe in yourself.

21. Life is (still) unfair.

22. Never too old.

23. May we be remembered.

1. INTRODUCTION

This book is written for seniors, potential seniors and the young, who think that they will never grow old. It may be disjointed, disorganized and rambling: the product of a clueless codger. I never liked long introductions. Play ball. Get to the point.

2. HANGING AROUND: HOW HAVE I LIVED SO LONG, YET LEARNT SO LITTLE?

I turned eighty-years-old on September 12th, 2015.

Less than half of our population reaches that age, so do I get credit for reaching eighty? What did I have to do with it? Should I be proud... or not?

I was substitute-teaching a few years ago, when a second-grader came up to my desk, looked at me and said: "You're getting old, huh?"

"Yeah, if you hang around long enough, that's what happens," I said.

"I know," he replied, "my father's getting old, too."

Now, we are not supposed to admit how old we are. Every time I tell some childhood story, my wife says that I'm showing my age. Well, I don't mind that at all - am I supposed to be ashamed of being old?

I used to think of seniors as living history – people with a lot of interesting stories to tell. My favorite old story (to

1

which nobody under sixty will relate) happened when I was about eight-years-old: I had an uncle who worked for the railroad; we children would be outside playing (can you believe that: *outside* playing?) when we would see him coming down the street toward us. We all got excited, because we knew that he would give us each a quarter.

In the early 1940s, here's what we did with twenty-five cents (are you seated?): we went to the movies for twelve cents, where we bought a box of candy for a nickel; after the show, we went to the ice-cream store and bought a cone for another nickel, leaving us three cents change. Today, all of that would cost a minimum of fifteen dollars!

My second favorite story happened to my wife's cousin, whom I used to visit weekly, in her assisted-living residence. Cousin Catharine, who died at age 99¾, grew up in New England, in the early 1900s. Her grandmother, then in her eighties, lived with Catharine's family. People were just starting to get electricity, and the electrician had just installed this wondrous new advancement in Catharine's house. Well, her grandmother would walk over to the electric switch on the wall, turn it on and glance up at the ceiling-light, with this incredulous expression on her face; then, she would repeat the movement, with the same reaction.

What hath God wrought?

She never once dreamed of computers, smart phones, i-Pads, e-mails or texting.

My uncle Joe also lived to be ninety-nine. He never smoked or drank alcohol, and I never heard him curse. He took good care of himself and ate the proper foods; he said that he chewed each bite of his food thirty-two times, because we have thirty-two teeth.

Now we have so many labels for the generations: the "Baby Boomers", the "Gen-Xers", the "Millennials"... and, what about us? Are we the "Geezennials"? I am not a spokesman for any group, and I certainly can't claim to be a spokesman just because my picture was on the cover of *GQ (Geezer Quarterly)* magazine, but at age eighty, I believe, contrary to popular advice, that we should eat anything we want, say anything we want and not worry about exercise.

My maternal grandmother was my outspoken model. Years ago, she hosted a baby-shower for my aunt, whose husband, Uncle Ernie, came to pick her up after the festivities. Grandma welcomed him with open arms and blurted out: "Ernie, Ernie, you look older than your father!"

Another time, this same Uncle Ernie was in heated conversation with my father - yelling seemed to be the standard form of conversation for Italian men in that era, and sitting there, I could not squeeze in a word for at least two hours. Finally, as Ernie took a deep breath, I offered a sentence. He turned and glared at me: "Anthony, would you mind not interrupting?"

*

So, when you reach eighty, you hope that maybe you have gained some wisdom. You also wonder why you have been spared, while so many others have not. And, you might even still think about your personal appearance.

In my case, I was always bothered by my double chin. My grandmother used to tell me to keep rubbing the skin there, to reduce its size, but it never worked. I thought about having some plastic surgery, as one of my cousins did - I even had the plastic-surgeon take a look and give me an estimate. As I pondered over the issue, it hit me: "I'm about to pay this doctor six-thousand dollars to cut my throat!" So, I decided to live with the flab.

So many of my boyhood friends have passed on. Many were fine athletes; my best-friend was an outstanding natural athlete: he loved baseball. He told the story of two baseball players, one a pitcher and one a second baseman: the second baseman passed away, and one night the pitcher dreamt about him.

"Do they have baseball in heaven?" asked the pitcher.

"Well, there's good news and bad news," answered the second baseman: "the good news is that, yes, there is baseball in heaven; the bad news is you're pitching next Tuesday."

3. HOW I GOT SO OLD

For better or worse, we are all born into our particular families.

I once read a debatable premise: that we choose our own parents. In my case, I was very lucky to be born into two loving, loud, Italian families - nine children on my father's side and six on my mother's. They lived around the corner from each other, two blocks from the nation's capital. Owning a car was completely unnecessary - we walked everywhere: the corner grocery store, the school, the church, the movies, the streetcar and the Boys' Club.

I never realized that the Boys' Club was for under-privileged children until about forty years later. It was founded by Miss Virginia Merrick, a wheelchair-bound woman, who is now proposed for sainthood by the Catholic church; we paid one-dollar a year for membership. I loved the Club, and never thought of myself as under-privileged - to the contrary, life was rich and full.

My father's father came from Reggio Calabria, Italy, in the early 1900s. They call Calabrians *"testa-dura"*, which means "hard-headed" (my wife says daily that I am living proof of this). My grandfather, Anastasi lived across the street from the church, where he attended daily mass and helped out. He also had a small altar of St. Anthony at his bedside.

Every day, for fifty years, Grandpa walked to work on the railroad at Union Station. He raised nine children, mostly on his own, because my grandmother was often sick. He had a fig tree and some vegetables in the backyard, and always made his own wine and Italian sausages. I spent many Friday nights with him, consuming some *scaloda* and *bacala*, and playing checkers (making sure that he would win - his hard-headedness ensured that he was always a winner).

Grandpa was a man of honor. His brother Joe, who arrived in New York first, was engaged to a woman named Concetta, who had travelled from Italy to the U.S. to marry him. But, sometime after Grandpa arrived, Joe broke off the engagement, so Grandpa took Concetta as his wife.

My mother's father, Grandpa Spigone, came from Segni, Italy, also in the early 1900s. Grandpa was a chef for the U.S. Senate, and created the famous bean

7

soup, still served in senate dining rooms today. Aunts, uncles and cousins abounded in the neighbourhood, and we were happy families back then - around the time of World War II - until misfortune devastated our families, when my mother passed away, aged thirty-five, whilst giving birth. I was nine-years-old and my brother Bob was five, but my dim memories still reveal the strong love I will always have for her.

My father, of course, was heartbroken, though eventually his sense of humor helped him to survive. He was an unintentionally funny man: he never tried to be - he just was. The only times he would wear a necktie were weddings and funerals. He would usually be running late for the events and would always tie it so that the bottom piece would come out longer than the top, so he would grab the scissors and cut the bottom part off. For Christmas one year, he opened his present and found a new necktie with a pair of scissors. Another of his habits was to apply a vinegar-soaked washcloth to his forehead, after an occasional night of one too many drinks with his brothers. So, another Christmas present included a washcloth, with a bottle of vinegar.

Soon after my mother's death,

Grandma Spigone took us in and cared for us, lovingly, for two years, until my father remarried. Grandma would rise early, shovel coal into the furnace, get us ready for school, and work hard all day for her immediate family, and for us. Every Thursday she would make homemade spaghetti and meatballs. She made her own sauce and homemade pasta from flour and eggs - I've never tasted anything so good in my life: Grandma baked the love right into the pasta. Each Sunday afternoon, after the meal was served and the kitchen was cleaned, Grandma took herself to the movies, and those two hours were hers alone.

During those two years, there was always some joyous excitement in my grandmother's house. My uncle, his wife and daughter lived on the top floor, my grandparents, two aunts, my brother and I slept in the second-floor bedrooms, while the first floor housed the kitchen, hall, furnace room and parlor (as it was called back then). Our aunts spoilt us with trips downtown, for a movie, stage-show and lunch - even in those days, we could afford some enjoyable things.

My brother, Bob, who was not enamored of school at the time (we had to bribe him with a nickel for candy, to get him to attend) later became a school-principal, and president of the Principals' Association. Today, my wondrous, loving brother and his wife, Wanda, are the two best parents and grandparents ever. And, as far as I know, this guy (unlike his brother) has never uttered a profane word: occasionally, he may say "sugar" instead of "sh—"

Bob and I remember an older, Italian man in the neighbourhood, who would take orders from neighbors for fresh Italian bread. He would board the streetcar with a big white sack, travel to the Italian bakery on North Capitol Street and return with bread. How can I describe this bread, which was better than any cake you could buy? With the bread still hot out of the oven, we would melt some butter on it and devour it, whilst singing: "Heaven, I'm in heaven..."

*

My present-day family is a source of great joy for me, and the most important part of my life.

My son, John, an avid guitarist, has struggled with depression for much of his life, but makes me proud for his tireless efforts. My eldest daughter, Marie-

Christine, is a wonderful mother, and has worked on humanitarian issues such as the Orphans and Vulnerable Children Initiative, as well as helping Syrian refugees. She and Joe, our dear son-in-law, have presented us with the priceless gift of our only grandchild, Keira Noelle. My middle daughter, Erin, works for the United Nations in New York, where she is acting-director of the U.N. Global Campaign to End Fistula, a life-threatening condition affecting many women in developing countries, who do not receive timely and appropriate care when giving birth. She also writes heart-wrenching poetry about the third-world. My youngest daughter, Jennifer, is a committed leader, trying to save our planet - her passion is business recycling and finding ways to befriend the Earth. My wife, Jeanne, works diligently to help her family, and also volunteers in helping others. She is still searching for her own mission on Earth, which I think maybe she has already found: without her, none of this aging tome would have been possible, since I know minus-zero about computers.

This reminds me that I need to try analyzing why I reject our digital technology age. I was recently in a wine-store, asking the young cashier if he carried a particular wine. He said no and advised me to look for it on the internet; I told him that I didn't have a computer. His whole being shook in astonishment, as he barked out: "How can you live?"

For some reason, I *can* live - and want to - without the digital revolution. Aside from being hacked by deviants and foreign countries, as well as the risk of losing your credit card, your identity or your life (as some young women have), my main reason is otherwise: I'm talking about it taking the human element out of our humanity. Are we becoming the very robots that we are trying to invent? What has happened to the human personal touch: the warm handshake and the often very-needed hug? What about the personal letter and the personal phone-call? And, do we really need the daily pile of e-mails? I long for the days when I would get a personal letter in the mail, instead of all the requests for monetary donations, or a pleasant personal phone-call from a friend, instead of the pestering telemarketing call. The young cashier in the wine-store is probably wondering how any of us can live without a computer, a Kindle, a tablet, a laptop, a smart-phone or a large-screen TV (note: here I am, using a computer to reject computers... but this is my wife's computer, so it's okay). How can we survive without these luxuries? I say to the young man in the wine-store: "Tell it to a Syrian refugee."

There is no going back - we cannot reverse "progress". But, I'm resisting, and trying to live my life as I did in the gloriously innocent days of the 1950s. Tom Brokaw named our World War II heroes as "the greatest generation", and I'm naming the 1950s as the greatest decade.

4. "YOU DID WHAT?"

Some of my earliest memories go back to St. Joseph's Elementary School, near the Capitol.

We played basketball before school, at recess and after school (we had no football team and I was lousy at baseball). We loved our coach, Father Farrell. He told my father that I had a "hawk-eye" for shooting. We also had the Boys' Club, where we could play all of the sports and attend summer camp for our one-dollar-a-year dues.

We would go to confession on Saturday and mass on Sunday. My cousin John and I sold newspapers after masses, in front of the church - sometimes we made a profit of three dollars. At Saturday confession, we never wanted to get in the line for the Monsignor, who intimidated us, both on and off the altar. One Saturday, my friend Joe and I were lined up, when an usher came over and ordered us to stand in the Monsignor's line.

"Let's get out of here," Joe said, as I pulled him back into line. But, in the sacred silence of the church, Joe stumbled into the confessional. After another moment of silence, we heard the Monsignor shout: "You did what!" Joe jumped up and ran out of the church in tears. I never did find out what he did, but I think that may have been his last confession.

At school, we would learn about "indulgences" granted by the church: there was a "partial" indulgence, which abolished some of your sins, and then there was a "plenary" indulgence, which set you free and cleaned the whole slate (recently, I was at a panel discussion on politics and faith, where one of the panellists wondered how much a "plenary" indulgence might bring on *eBay* these days).

After a few years at St. Joseph's, our family moved from DC to Silver Spring, MD, where I attended St. Michael's grade school. I was chosen as 8th grade president and valedictorian, although, as a new student, I don't know why. My teacher, Sister Maria Patricia, wrote an eight-page speech for me to memorize and deliver at graduation - with a little stumble, I got through it.

I enjoyed playing basketball there, but what I liked most was a game we played at weekend parties. Too advanced for "spin the bottle", we played this new game called "flash": one person used a flashlight to scan the darkened room, trying to catch a couple kissing. When caught, the kisser would exchange places with the flashlight searcher, and this would continue (endlessly, I hoped), as partners had ample time to check each other out; since we didn't have computer-dating back then, it was a great idea. Otherwise, I was much too shy to try kissing a girl on my own.

I did get up my courage once. Our basketball team was on a train ride to Philadelphia, to play a game there. My team-mate Jimmy, a year older than most of us, was our guru on matters of girls. Jimmy was seated across from me, with his arm around his girlfriend, and I was sitting next to my own girlfriend, with my hands in my lap. Jimmy kept motioning to me to put my arm around her; after many moments of mental struggling, I slowly floated my arm around her and felt like a king.

One day after school, I was playing softball when a new neighborhood kid named Leonard showed up. After we welcomed him, he mentioned that he had gone to Kenilworth Elementary School, where I had attended kindergarten, before St. Joseph's. He said that on the first day of kindergarten he was called into the principal's office for hitting a classmate in the eye with a stone. I was speechless: *I was that kid.* As we struggled through our teens we enjoyed activities together, but he was to become a sort of lifetime jinx to me: he drove my first car into a creek, installed parts backwards in it, and recklessly sped his own car into an accident, causing me a deviated septum, among other mishaps. When he came to my house to apologize, the handle to the front-door came off in his hand. We remained friends for many years, until the last jinx.

5. MEN DEVOTE MUCH OF THEIR LIVES...

Some days, after school, my best friend John and I would have our little talks.

We agreed that the two most beautiful things in the world are the TRUTH, and a woman's anatomy. I write "truth" in capital letters because although it is so beautiful and powerful, you may seldom see it. We also decided that women, in general, are the better sex, hands down. We found it so fascinating that men devote much of their lives scheming to re-enter the female anatomy, that once housed men's original sanctum.

*

From St. Michael's, I went on to Gonzaga High School, in DC, where the Jesuit priests had authority to slap you around if necessary, and to order a minimum of at least three hours of homework a night.

One day I went home and told my stepmother that the priest had hit me. She promptly called the priest, requesting a repeat performance: "Hit him again - he needs it."

On a typical school day, I would take the bus from Silver Spring to the DC line, and then take a streetcar downtown, where I would transfer to another one, travel a few miles and walk four blocks to school. I was always working on the school newspaper or yearbook after school, so I would get home around five-thirty, have dinner, do my homework and go to bed.

One yearbook experience in particular comes to mind: my friend, Jim Kane, played tight-end on the football team, and I got an exciting action shot of him diving through the air, into the end-zone. I knew that Jim was aching for me to use this photo in the yearbook, so I held this over his head and took full advantage of it, for most of the school year. Jim was most willing to do my bidding, buy my lunch and generally see what my latest wish was. I still see Jim on occasion, and he still speaks to me.

I wanted bigger things: I yearned to write sports for the *Washington Daily News*. So, I pestered our school correspondent to the paper to take me there with him - he finally gave in. I remember trying to write my first story: I sat down to write with a pencil and pad...

"No, no," the editor said, "you must type it out." Well, Gonzaga never offered a typing course - you could study Latin, Greek and religion, but not typing. So, I started pecking away with one finger, then eventually two fingers, as I do now. It was such a thrill for a kid to watch in excitement, as the newspapers roared off the presses, and I would grab a copy, searching for my bye-lined piece. Later, I would board the bus home, watching for any passengers who might be reading my story.

Going to an all-boys' school, with no girls in sight, we had to create our own fun. I had a wonderful Greek teacher - Father Suppe - who twirled an imaginary moustache and puffed on a piece of chalk. During exams, he would scan us like a hawk, looking for anyone with "crib (cheat) notes". As he scoured the room during one exam, I saw him look at me, as I was peering inside my coat jacket.

"A-ha, Mr. Anastasi!" he yelled, as he raced toward me. Pulling me out of the seat by my necktie, he reached into my inside coat pocket and yanked out the piece of paper, which read:

"April Fool!"

After school that day, I was sentenced to do time in *"JUG"* (only at a

Jesuit institution could detention be called "Justice Under God"!).

In my freshman year at Gonzaga, I met a classmate named Bill Iglehart. Today, he would be labelled a "nerd" or "geek", but Bill was a brilliant student, with a vocabulary just short of William F. Buckley's. Some students made fun of Bill, but I always enjoyed talking to him, because I would always learn some new words. For example, one day, I asked: "Bill, have you ever been sent to *JUG*?"

He answered: "On various occasions I have been susceptible to breaches of disciplinary convention." I just stood there, in awe of this fourteen-year-old linguist.

I think that I was a born prankster, but my friends at Gonzaga also pulled some good ones on me. In senior year, I bought an old car and parked in the school parking-lot. After class one day I went out to get my car, which was nowhere in sight - I thought it was stolen. Then, as I walked down the driveway to North Capitol Street, what did I see in the middle of the streetcar tracks? My friends had released the brake and coasted it all the way down the driveway, onto the street. Luckily, it remained a harmless little prank.

One other time, I was in the senior

21

lounge, located two storeys up from the ground. My pals placed my suit-jacket out on the ledge, and when I climbed out of the window onto the ledge to get it, they locked the window shut (with friends like this, right..?). A sympathetic classmate allowed me back in.

The following summer, my father, who was a stonemason, got me a job loading and unloading trucks full of stone in a quarry, for seventy-five cents an hour - this quickly inspired me to go on to college! One other summer job was even more unprofitable: I drove an ice-cream truck, six days a week, from ten a.m. to ten p.m. Popsicles cost a nickel and many of the kids had only a few pennies, so I would let it slide; the lock on the back of the truck was also broken, causing products to disappear. So, after working for them for twelve days, the company called to tell me that I owed them $7.20. More reason to head to college.

6. "AIN'T THIS TUESDAY?"

After Gonzaga I went on to the University of Maryland, at College Park, where I continued my journalism experience by becoming sports-editor of the campus newspaper, *The Diamondback*, and by doing the color commentary on basketball games, for the campus radio-station.

One of my columns about the football-team was not too popular with the teammates. "They came here looking for you last night," the editor told me; "it's a good thing that you weren't here." At first I agreed, but then I thought about how it would have made an exciting story, had I been there to take a blow for the team.

I fondly remember my two best pranks in college:

A friend had an early History class one day, and I had nothing to do, so I sat in, in the last seat in the row, next to the door. This was a Monday, Wednesday and Friday class, but such a large class that I figured I'd never be noticed. As the professor began to take roll, I tried to slouch down. Eventually, he looked at me:

"I don't seem to have you on my roster."

Knowing no better, I stood up, scratched my head, and said: "Ain't this Tuesday?" The class roared, as I ran out of the classroom, with the teacher's words ringing in my ears: "Come back! Come back!"

I was an English major and Professor Brennan taught one of my classes. One day, coming into class, I noticed a message on the blackboard: "There will be no class today", signed by "Professor Brennan". The following week, I was the first to arrive early, before class, so I wrote on the blackboard: "No class today", imitating his signature (don't let your children read this).

My favorite class was Shakespeare, for two semesters, presented by Dr. Zeeveld – each class was like going to see a different play: Dr. Z would act out the scenes and, as the scene ended, the bell would ring, as he walked off stage.

7. "LEFT... RIGHT... LEFT..."

I was scheduled to graduate in June, but Uncle Sam had other ideas for me: the letter came in the spring, requesting my presence in the U.S. army in May. I was fortunate to be drafted during the period after the Korean War, and before Vietnam.

So, I went off to Fort Jackson, SC, and received my diploma in the mail later. Generally, the army was an enjoyable adventure, except for the eight weeks of basic training. I was among the one-percent who actually liked army food.

Our drill-instructor was the aptly named Sergeant Finger, a good ol' boy from Georgia, who loved to assert his newfound authority. I got caught on the first day for not having shaved that morning - Sgt. Finger got in my face, nose-to-nose, yelling: "Anastasi, you look like shit, boy!" I had to stand on a platform, in front of the whole company, and dry-shave, without water or shaving cream - one of the more unforgettable moments of my basic training.

Another such moment occurred on a

fifteen-mile march through sand, on a ninety-five-degree day, carrying our rifles and backpacks, but no water. I think I had an out-of-body experience that day, because I knew that couldn't really be me there, on that march. When we finally got to the end, sadistic Sgt. Finger was standing next to a large lister bag of cool water.

"Any of you boys thirsty?" he asked, as he emptied all of the water out onto the sand. "It'll make a man out of you." Or, it will just make you very thirsty.

Back at the barracks the next morning, Sgt. Finger gave the order, in standard army lingo: "I want to see thirty-two swinging dicks on that blacktop in twenty seconds. Does everyone understand?!"

After Fort Jackson, I was lucky to get really good, exciting assignments: my first was working at the Pentagon on *Pentagram News*, co-writing singer Steve Lawrence's Saturday morning radio show, working on the retirement of General Maxwell Taylor, chair of the Joint Chiefs of Staff, and participating in planning the funeral of Secretary of State John Foster Dulles. One of my real treats in Washington was thanks to an army friend, whose grandmother, Victoria Geaney, was official hostess of Blair House, the President's guesthouse. Ms. Geaney was so kind to us, showing us her little Sputnik memento from Russia's Nikita Khrushchev, as well as the rooms where heads of state stayed, including Queen Elizabeth and Charles DeGaulle. I was addicted to cigars at the time, and the lovely Ms. Geaney presented me with some of the special cigars they stocked for Winston Churchill's visits.

One night, before we left Blair House, we enjoyed playing poker, next to the first-floor dumb-waiter. Even better than the poker winnings were the delightful dinner items coming down on the dumb-waiter, with champagne left over from the Secretary of State's dinner party, on the main floor.

8. "YOU LITTLE &*$%#&! I'LL KILL YOU!"

After the Army, I returned to my sports-writing job at the Washington Daily News.

I got to cover boxing, which I loved, having grown up watching three matches a week with my father. I covered a lightweight championship match, featuring Paolo Rossi and Joe Brown, and a ferocious middleweight bout, featuring Joey Giardello (who later became middleweight champion). Joey asked me if I could arrange for him and his family to meet President Eisenhower. I didn't know any better, so I called the White House with his request, and they told me that Ike was in Europe, and asked would we instead like to meet Vice-President Nixon.

So, we all went to his office in the Capitol building and were very impressed with him. Nixon was a big sports fan, and had been a member of his college football team. He had done his homework for this insignificant little meeting with us, and he sat astride his desk - not in a chair - as he recited Joey's boxing record. We took pictures and left, symbolizing six more votes for Mr. Nixon.

The following week I went to the Casino Royal nightclub in DC, to meet Walter Winchell and Bobby Darin (I promise not to drop too many more names on you); after the performance, the three of us strolled around town. Years later, I heard of the tragic ending to Mr. Winchell's life, when he (one of America's foremost journalists) was blackballed, before suffering an untimely death.

Back at the *News*, I was assigned to write daily bowling stories. One day, I came in and discovered there was no bowling news in my mailbox - the night-editor told me that a colleague had come in earlier, tore up the bowling news and trashed it. So, I dug it out and wrote the bowling column. Now, how was I to straighten out my colleague, who disliked bowling and only wanted major sports appearing in our newspaper? I phoned a local bowling lane and asked the manager if they would like to name one of their bowling teams after my destructive colleague - he said they would be happy to oblige; the next day's sports-section featured a story about my colleague's new bowling team.

Not everybody liked this - "Mr. Big

Sports" arrived looking for me, and as he approached, I could see the steam from his nostrils, his face reddening; "You little &*$ %#&! You do that again and I'll kill you!" I never did it again.

9. "WOMAN OF THE YEAR"

Unfortunately, the *News* went out of business in the 1960s, as did many other publications. So, I joined the federal government, where I wrote press-releases, feature-stories, pamphlets and speeches (which I did by default, because no-one else wanted to).

My biggest story was about Dr. Nina Braunwald, the first certified female heart-surgeon in the U.S. The story was published internationally, with Dr. Braunwald featured as *Life* magazine's *"Woman of the Year"*.

My big prank, working at the National Institutes of Health, was on my boss, who was chief of their public information program. Every Thursday, we would have a weekly meeting of all of the NIH Public Information Officers; on one occasion, I arranged for my friend to phone my boss's office during the meeting, posing as Nixon's pressman, Herb Klein, and requesting a full report from every institute, on all of its activities; then, after the meeting, my boss would return to his office, read the phone-call message, and I would pop in, yelling: "April Fool!"

Well, of course, the whole thing backfired! When the call came in, my boss's secretary thought it so important that she immediately delivered it to him in the meeting. I was in shock, as he announced the White House "assignment" to the group, knowing it was too late for me to jump in. That night, somewhat sleepless, I tried to decide what I should do: should I tell the truth, and possibly lose my job, or keep quiet? I decided to tell the truth.

The following day, walking sheepishly into my boss's office, I told him what I had done, and braced myself for his response.

Remaining the wonderful, kind man that he was, he smiled, said that he understood, and concluded that maybe all of those reports would come in handy, someday. What a treasure: to have such a great boss.

But, let me not forget my first wonderful boss at NIH, Mr. Lea Martin. During my first week there, I approached Mr. Martin with a question. He placed his hand on my shoulder and said: "Tony, why don't you go out and play a little golf, and we'll talk about it tomorrow?"

From NIH, I went to work at the

National Alcohol Institute, where I wrote speeches for the director and developed a newsletter I called *Speakeasy* (despite my boss's objections). I was also assigned to write some political speeches, as well as the Mother's Day Address for President Gerald Ford.

The director of the Alcohol Institute was a loud man, who sometimes almost seemed to be under the influence himself. Sometimes, he looked at my drafts and said: "Oh, this looks good, Tony." Other times he would spurt out: "Who wrote this piece of crap?" To cope with the bureaucracy, I had my own special filing system: an inbox, an outbox and a *googooza* box (named for the southern Italian slang, which means "butt" or "rear-end").

I would go out for lunch almost every day, rather than eating at my desk. But, one day our secretary was off sick, so I stayed in to answer the phones. A man called to speak to a colleague who was busy at the time, so we started to chat.

"What do you do there?" he asked. "I'm looking for someone who can write speeches and press releases."

I replied: "That's what I'm doing."

"Come on in for an interview," he

said. I interviewed the next day and got the job, which was a big promotion. Is it better to be lucky or to have talent? Maybe some of both help.

Meanwhile, I was in the process of meeting my future wife, whom I thought was "geographically desirable", because we worked in the same building. Well, not only couldn't I get to first base with her, I couldn't even get out of the dugout! After six months, I did get to hold her hand! Before I could progress, a close friend surprised me:

I was living in a small studio apartment, when the phone rang, one Saturday morning: my friend was outside in the parking lot, with all of his earthly belongings in the car - he asked if I would take him in. I said yes, and we ended up getting a bigger place for two years, and having some good times, before I married.

Time for just one more prank:

Now married and living in our first home, in the seventies, our next-door neighbor decided to uproot the dead tree in his front yard. He tied a rope to the tree and the other end to his car's back bumper, and shortly thereafter, the tree was yanked from the ground, and ended up lying in the street, along with his back bumper. I had assumed after that he had disposed of the tree, but the following day, as I was driving down the road, I spotted it dumped in a nearby field. I tucked the tree into my car's trunk, then later, in the dark of night, I crept over into his front yard, replanting it in the same exact space he had removed it from. The next morning, I couldn't wait to see his face. I think he suspected me though, and he wouldn't come out, to let me enjoy the satisfaction of my venture.

However, we remained friends. He was always encouraging me to run for office in the Senior Flatulence Society (SFS), or the neighborhood Senior Sauntering Society (SSS). I lost the SFS race to a much louder fellow and was outpaced for the SSS position. So, I decided to spend some spare time mentoring local, third-grade children - what better activity could I pursue?

My grandparents shortly after their arrival from Italy:
Grandpa Anastasi, Grandma Concetta, Aunt Mary, my father
Anthony (Nino) and Aunt Angie.

My mother and father, Virginia and Nino Anastasi.

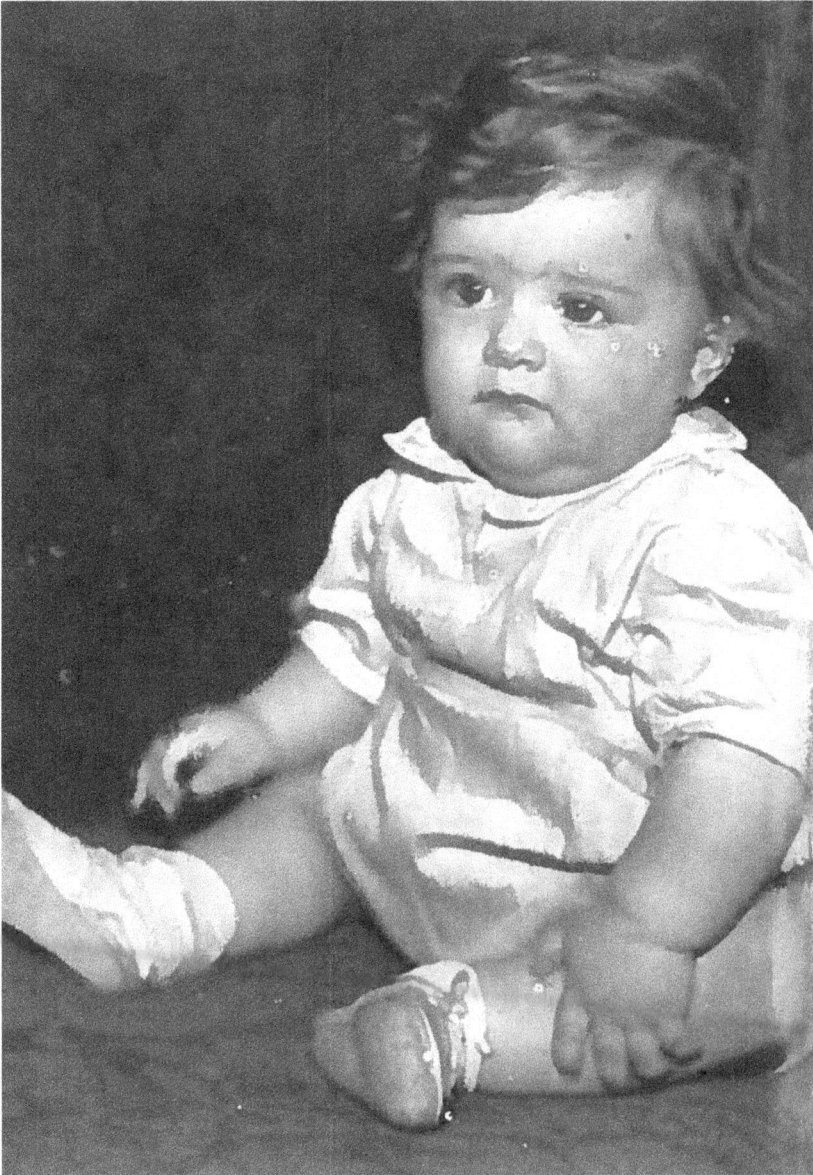

Me at five months old,
with the same bewildered expression he has to this day:
"What's it all about?"

Me the basket-ball player at seventeen
(too short for the NBA).

1970s family photo: Me with wife Jeanne (seated) and daughters
(left to right) Jennifer, Erin and Marie-Christine.

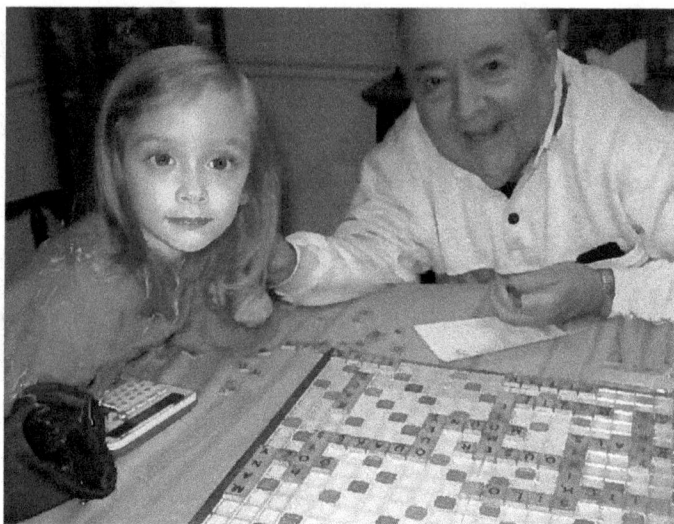

My granddaughter Keira beats me at Scrabble, again.

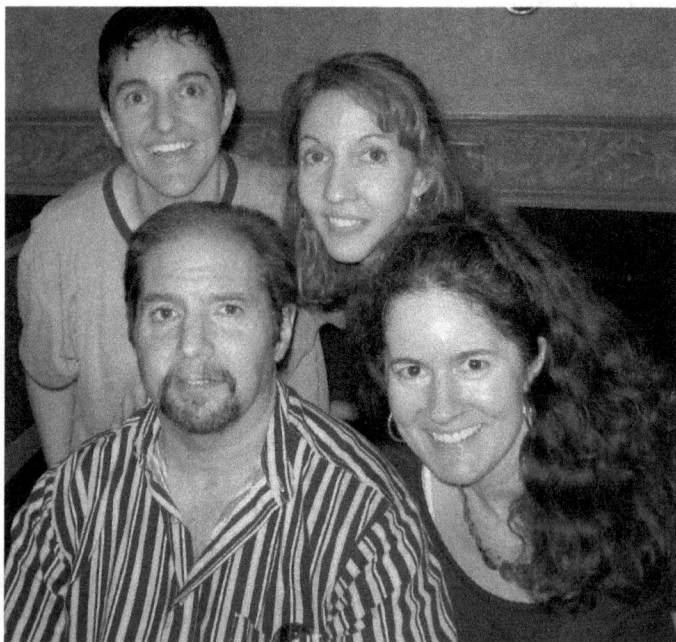

My four children: John, Jennifer, Marie-Christine, Erin

10. AGING NOT NECESSARILY RELATED TO DISEASE

Now, what about our health?

America's longest running scientific study of aging started in 1958 and is still being conducted by the National Institute on Aging: the program is called the "Baltimore Longitudinal Study of Aging", and is world-renowned for its major contributions on the aging process. Two major conclusions have surfaced from this study: first, the changes which occur with aging do not necessarily lead to disease, though, conversely, some of the health problems experienced during aging result from disease processes, rather than from the natural process of aging. Second, no single chronological timetable exists for human aging: we all age differently.

We all know by now that exercise and proper eating contribute to good health. But, even though we may have good health, we should make sure that we have a valid will, before it's too late. My father-in-law was a lawyer, and he died without a will!

It's understandable why we don't like

to talk about wills and death. I feel the same way that Woody Allen does about death: I'm not afraid of dying - I just don't want to be there when it happens. Woody is eighty now and I wish he wouldn't worry about it so much; maybe he could talk to his rabbi, or somebody who has died and come back.

Which also reminds me of funerals. I love the story about the old Italian man on his deathbed, who suddenly gets a whiff of his favorite cookies, coming out of the oven, which his loving wife has prepared and is now setting out on the kitchen table. The man fumbles out of his bed, struggles to the stairs and crawls down to the kitchen, but just as he is about to stretch out his hand and grab a cookie, his wife slaps his hand with a spatula, and growls: "Those are for the funeral."

On a more serious note, let me try to describe the old Italian funerals. After the death, the family schedules viewings from two to four, and from seven to nine, for three straight days - the funeral follows, after the third day. In all, the mourning and emotional toll are dragged out for four days! I much prefer a new, modern approach: the decedent's body is placed in the rear of the church, where relatives and friends come to pay their last respects; this takes place in late-morning, after which the church service is conducted. The final step is the drive to the cemetery. Everything is wrapped up, all in one day, hopefully providing fewer burdens on the family. Of course, there is the option of cremation, which is quick and far less expensive - this choice appears to be somewhat of a modern trend.

I've been to a number of viewings over the years, and there have been some things which bothered me at times, which I will come to shortly.

But first, I'm reminded of a movie, in which a number of Italian relatives and friends are shown passing by a coffin, individually. The women are all dressed in traditional black, some crying and some clutching the casket. As the men pay their respects, one old *compadre* bends forward, peering into the coffin, and spits on the decedent; some say this may be a typical reaction from some Italians. His rationale was that if the man was not worthy whilst alive, then death does not improve his image.

11. TELL HIM (HER) NOW

One thing, especially, bothered me at some of these viewings: I'm sitting there, listening to people saying: "Oh, why didn't I honor him, and tell him that I loved him, while he was alive?"

An excellent point. Why don't many of us do just that? Right now? If there are special ones that we love or respect, I think it is vitally important to tell them, whilst they can still hear and appreciate it - we have the time and the chance to do it now.

One other comment I hear a lot at viewings: when looking at the decedent, someone says: "Oh, he looks so good." Well, I've seen him looking better!

But, really, what can one say, but the same old platitudes. I think that the best gift we can offer is our presence.

I believe that all of us over fifty should take Bill Clinton's advice, which he shared during a TV interview, a few years ago: Clinton advised seniors to write about their life-history, for their families and for posterity. It can be therapeutic and also provide an insight into your life, for your children and grandchildren. I remember, years ago, doing an amateur interview with a friend's grandfather; years later, the family treasured the tape.

At eighty, maybe you start thinking about putting words onto paper, whilst you are (hopefully) still in a partially sound state of mind. You look at the obit page, realize that you're going to be there someday, and start to wonder where, when and how. You think about ways in which you can wisely use whatever time you have left.

12. THE VALUE OF SECOND AND THIRD OPINIONS

In matters of health, always get a second or third opinion. That's important to say, first off - I wouldn't be here otherwise.

I had a deviated septum (as the result of Leonard the jinx's auto accident), so I went in for the doctor to take a look at it. He had barely looked, before trying to get me to sign the papers for surgery. I told him that I would first get a second opinion (many doctors don't like that). I went to the second doctor who, by coincidence, happened to be the first doctor's partner, though he practiced across town. Number two took a look and asked me if I could live with it, instead. I said that I had been told the invasive procedure was only minor surgery; I'll never forget his words, as he looked me squarely in the eye, and said: "No surgery is minor." Thanks to his honesty, to this day I'm living with the deviated septum.

In another example, I have had chronic back-pain since my teenage years, as a result of working in the stone quarry.

Like I said, that experience was the best wake-up call I could ever imagine for enrolling in college: I knew I couldn't spend the rest of my life hauling stone. I have been helped by chiropractors (no, they're not quacks) and other health professionals; one M.D. was giving me injections in the back with a very long needle, which I thought might go through the table - others were giving me various back procedures. Until, I finally found a doctor who did an x-ray, which showed that it was not my back which was ailing, but my hip, because of a lack of cartilage. So, I had the hip replacement, which still serves me well in this new decade of life.

My third example happened about a decade ago, when I had a colonoscopy. The doctor called me into his office afterwards, showed me a chart of the colon, and said: "We're going to have to remove part of your colon." The problem was not really that I had polyps, but more so that one particular polyp was wrapped around a delicate part of the colon, necessitating very intricate surgery.

I thought to myself: *Well, it's time for a second opinion again.* So, I asked around for a good "second-opinion man", and I kept coming up with the same name: Dr. Lee Smith, at Washington Hospital

Center, who removed the polyp expertly, without needing to remove part of my colon. To this day, I have him to thank for saving this English major from becoming a "semi-colon".

In recent years, I've had a few more colonoscopies. Nowadays, they have something new for seniors: with a typical colonoscopy, you have to fast, drinking some kind of (semi-poisonous) liquid the day before, whilst stationing yourself within short flatulence from the toilet.

When you reach your seventies and eighties, there is a balance between a colonoscopy - which could possibly damage your aging colon - and just doing a stool sample via Cologuard, which reportedly discovers ninety-percent of cancerous polyps. The same goes for prostate problems with older men: when you hit eighty, they realize that prostate cancer is usually slow-growing, so they often just let it go (probably thinking: *What do you want? You've already lived more than most people, so go ahead and get your things in order.*).

So, now I see my family doctor every three months, take two eye-drops every day (because of unsuccessful cataract surgery, by a non-board-certified ophthalmologist), daily pravastatin, vitamin-D and a baby aspirin.

13. SLEEPLESS IN ROCKVILLE

My main health concern lately has been a breathing problem, which interferes with my sleep. Now I understand why sleep deprivation is a form of torture, used in wartime.

What happens is that I sometimes struggle to take a deep breath, like trying to climb a mountain, but just not being able to get over the top. I went to three pulmonologists and none of them could really solve the puzzle.

I've had five sleep-studies in all: my first was years ago, in Chevy Chase; the second study was in Baltimore, when I couldn't get to sleep at all. I wasn't getting enough air, so I rang for the nurse - she came in and said: "We can't give you more air until you get to sleep."

I replied: "I can't get to sleep until I get more air (*Catch-22*)." So, at six a.m., I drove home from Baltimore, half-dazed.

Recently, I made an exciting discovery: I had just about given up on a good night's sleep, when I discovered a physician who is both a sleep specialist *and* a pulmonologist, which I think is just what I needed. He scheduled me for an overnight sleep-study in an attractive, spacious, private room.

The problem is that the technician attaches wires to your body, from head to foot, places a mask on your face, and then tells you to go to sleep, which is a real challenge, considering how uncomfortable you are. This was my fifth (and, I hope, final) sleep-study. If you don't need one, don't do it.

In this latest study, the nurse said that I did very well on the C-PAP machine, which provides continuous air for breathing. They also have a Bi-PAP machine, which I wanted to try, but you have to use the C-PAP first, because the Bi-PAP is more expensive, and the insurance company wants you to have the cheaper one first. A week after the sleepover, the sleep doctor asked me back in, to discuss the results and to recommend the appropriate pressure for my C-PAP. But, I could never make friends with my C-PAP, so it now sleeps under my bed, and I'm using a nasal strip and a trazodone pill to help me sleep; I usually sleep for two to three hours at a time.

In fact, I was just now about to take a pill, when it fell to the floor, and I mean off the face of the Earth! It's got to be here, somewhere close by, but forget it: I'll never find it.

14. "IS ANYBODY UP THERE GOING TO HELP ME?"

I thought maybe my sleep problems needed divine intervention.

I started to pray for help, so frustrated one day that I looked up, pointed to the sky, and cried out: "Is anybody up there going to help me?" I did not get, nor expect, a verbal reply, but I kept praying.

I'm not saying that it was the prayers which helped, but all I know is that my breathing and sleeping have gradually improved (thank you, Somebody Up There). Since that time, I have also been doing some deep-breathing exercises and trying to do a little aerobic exercise, by getting out of my lazy-boy and walking around the ball-field.

Aside from sleeping, what about hearing? I know many people who have hearing-aids and, like me, don't use them. Why is this? What is it about hearing-aids that makes people ignore them? In my case, I'm too lazy to take the time required for maintenance, cleaning, new batteries, filters, etc. And, also, the way the world is today, I'm not sure that I want to hear about everything.

Big Pharma presents a major concern for seniors. I'm lucky, taking only a few meds, with good health-insurance cover. But, many of us are forced to pay astronomical prices for drugs, while the companies take the money and move overseas, to avoid paying their fair share of taxes - forcing U.S. citizens to pay more than their share. Recently, the young CEO of a pharmaceutical company attempted to gouge cancer patients with an exorbitant increase in the cost of certain cancer drugs and, in one of the few bipartisan attempts to reach across the senate aisle, legislators convened hearings to question the CEO of a company which increased the cost of life-saving EpiPens by five-hundred-percent, whilst that CEO was pulling a salary of eighteen-million dollars.

Another related health matter is dental care, which can be very costly. Good coverage with reasonable premiums is hard to find, although there is some basic coverage for those with disabilities, or on a low income.

A vital aspect of senior health involves care-givers. I have not experienced this yet, but it must be one of life's hardest tasks. I only have knowledge of this from movies and health articles, but we can all sympathize with them, wish them well, and help out wherever possible.

15. MAKING CONNECTIONS

Not to be overlooked is a crucial element in maintaining senior health: namely, connecting with others.

In corporate terms, we call this "networking"; in health terms, we describe it as a genuine interest in the well-being of others. Many seniors seem to be somewhat isolated, but there are so many ways for seniors to stay busy and avoid loneliness, which is hazardous to our health: we can do volunteer work, join Big Brothers or Big Sisters, mentor school-children, play sports in Senior Olympics, and allow our Senior Centers to continue spoiling us. If you can't find something to do, call me and we'll play checkers, Scrabble, or Boggle.

An extreme opposite of an isolated senior is a friend of mine, named Ted Murphy. A tough sports competitor, at the age of ninety-two, he's won a chest full of gold medals in the Senior Olympics. He was high-jumping and throwing the javelin in his eighties, and this year he'll be competing in bowling, ping-pong, bocce ball, and the discus throw. Ted's wife, Shirley, is also ninety-two. She is both an artist and an art-teacher, studies Spanish and reads literature, voraciously, as does Ted. They are too busy to get sick.

Ted has been my role-model since I met him twelve years ago, at bowling. My first time there I scored a 188 - he's such an all-out competitor that he wanted to know who got that high game, and we've been competing ever since. He's usually up around seven or eight a.m., golfing or playing bocce, while I'm reclining with my newspaper.

Sometimes, try as we might, we just can't make a connection. We recently went to a friend's house for dinner - the house was beautiful and the dinner was delicious. Our friend's brother-in-law was seated next to me at the table, so I was trying to engage his interest by asking various questions, such as: "Are you retired? What kind of work did you do? How do you spend your retirement time?" Despite my efforts, he never asked me one question about myself for the entire evening - I was baffled.

It reminds me of a Thanksgiving meal, many years ago, when I was sitting at dinner, with a group of relatives. Someone asked me where I was working at that time, and I replied: "The White House." I thought that someone might follow up by asking: "Oh, what do you do there?" But, all I heard was: "Would you please pass the mashed potatoes?" as everyone continued to enjoy their meal.

16. DAILY ROUTINE

I guess most of us have some kind of a daily routine.

I usually awaken around nine a.m. (if I'm breathing properly and returning to sleep after breaks). I then take my two eye-drops and have some coffee, reading the morning newspaper. I have breakfast, shower, shave and prepare to leave the house before noon, for some daily planned activity: Mondays I bowl (sometimes) and have my mentoring session with a third-grader at four-thirty; Tuesdays are my long days at "the office" - playing Scrabble, from noon to five-thirty, having dinner and playing poker until nine p.m. (is this my long day's journey into night?); Wednesdays can be bocce ball, ping-pong and a visit to my granddaughter; Thursdays are for bowling and poker again; Fridays are for grocery shopping, shooting pool and (hopefully) more ping-pong. I'm planning to work in a weekly visit to a local nursing home soon.

I almost forgot one of the things I enjoy most in my daily routine, whenever I get the chance: shuffleboard. A few years ago, Ted convinced me to participate in the Senior Olympics, so I entered the shuffleboard competition and won the first-place gold medal. Later, when I was telling some friends about my accomplishment, showing off my gold medal, of course they asked which sport I played. When I said shuffleboard, they couldn't control their laughter, until I pointed out to them that shuffleboard can be a contact sport: the fellow next to you can bump you with his walker and throw you off!

There is one thing that I have been trying to do in recent years: no matter who it is – the letter carrier, the grocery clerk, the waitress or a neighbor – I will try to find something positive to say to them: a kind word, a compliment and a smile. I fully agree with whoever it was that said we are all experiencing our daily battle with life, so why make it worse, when it is so easy to make it better? Sometimes a simple smile or pleasant word is enough.

After shopping at the supermarket recently, I was standing outside with my grocery cart, when an attractive young woman walked toward me and offered a very pleasant smile; I was pleased to return her smile, as she entered the store. A minute later, she returned and said to me:

"Thank you very much for smiling at me - I smile at so many people who never smile back."

Later, I thought (you always think of something good to say later) that I should have said: "Young lady, you remind me of a verse from an old Tony Bennett song: *'Beautiful girl, walk a little slower when you walk by me'*." Even at eighty, it is always possible to appreciate beauty, even if physical prowess has diminished.

17. AHH, THE OLD DAYS

Recently, John Kelly of *The Washington Post* - who writes an interesting daily column on local events - wrote a piece on "other-people talkers". These are usually seniors who want to talk or tell a story, whether you want to hear it or not.

When you're older, and have some years of experience, you often talk to whoever is around. When I do this, the conversation will trigger stories from the past, which I enjoy telling. One story leads to another - "that reminds me of...." - until eventually somebody quietens you down.

Many of us seniors enjoy talking about "the old days". I recently paid twenty-six dollars for two hamburgers, and it prompts me to share with our young people what it was like living back in the fifties. Our youth should know that there was a time in the USA when middle-class people could not only survive, but could sometimes thrive. I can remember paying ten cents for a hamburger at the Little Tavern shops - they were small, but very tasty; they also sold by the bagful of twelve for a dollar. I had a part-time job, making $1.60 per hour, whilst going to college, where the annual tuition was around five-hundred dollars a year! With my skimpy earnings I could afford to pay my own tuition, buy an old car for a hundred dollars, and still have a little spending money. I remember paying $25,000 for a brand-new house in the early sixties, and two-thousand cash for a new car, in 1972. Levitt was building new three-bedroom ramblers for $13,000 and, unbelievably, I put fifty dollars down on one of these, and they held it until I had made my decision.

We would never have imagined computers or the internet, and we had our own sources of entertainment. The early days of television started in the late forties - before that, we used our imaginations, listening to popular radio shows.

Sunday nights were a big time for the old radio shows: Bob Hope, Fred Allen and Phil Harris. The first big star of TV was the comedian Milton "Uncle Milty" Berle. But, by far the funniest, most entertaining show was *Amos and Andy* (also later on TV). Another top-rated show starred a Catholic priest, Bishop Fulton J. Sheen, whose show was "co-produced by his guardian angel".

What's worth watching on TV today?

For the best news analysis and commentary, we used to have Edward R. Murrow, Eric Sevareid, and Bill Moyers of *CBS News*; now we have Charlie Rose of *CBS* and Brian Lamb of *Public TV*.

Charlie is in a class by himself, with vast knowledge of multiple subjects, penetrating questions and a sincere search for the truth, in his daily interviews.

The retirement of Bill Moyers was a devastating blow to fans of his excellent intellectual programs.

In one, Bill tells the story of his White House years, with President Lyndon B. Johnson:

One evening, the President asked Bill to say grace before a White House dinner.

Bill proceeded, as the President bellowed, "Talk louder, Bill, we can't hear you."

Bill quickly responded: "I wasn't speaking to you, Mr. President."

18. THE RESUME AND THE EULOGY

David Brooks, the excellent *New York Times* columnist, and columnist Mark Shields, discuss weekly politics on the *PBS News Hour*, on Fridays.

Brooks has authored a popular book, titled: *The Road to Character*, in which he distinguishes "resumé virtues" from "eulogy virtues". *Resumé* virtues comprise a person's skills and career accomplishments, whereas *eulogy* virtues describe the spirit and characteristics of a person, as might be described at the person's funeral – two very different categories, which both give pause for thought. The eulogy, especially, reminds me of the old adage that nobody on his or her deathbed probably ever said: "I wish I had spent more time in the office." So, Brooks is encouraging each of us to search for something more - something far deeper than career highlights.

Brooks is one of my favorite thinkers and writers, but I must say that if I only have time to read one person's article, it must be columnist Michael Gerson, of *The*

Washington Post. His profound intellectual insights, sensitivity and spirituality are a reader's delight.

Another well-known TV news person, David Gregory, also seems to be on a spiritual journey. Recently, I heard him at Georgetown University, where he discussed his new book, *How's Your Faith?*, the title based on a quip by former President George W. Bush.

Gregory told how his ego was punctured when *NBC* relieved him of his duties, as moderator of *Meet the Press*. Feeling very down about this, he opened an encouraging note from a colleague which, in part, read: "We always knew you were unstoppable." Gregory pondered the meaning of this: did unstoppable mean that he had run roughshod over co-workers, pushing forward and thinking only of himself? He considered that he had perhaps been selfish, not considering the plans and feelings of others; this experience has directed him toward a more spiritual path, seeking knowledge from some of the world's foremost spiritual leaders.

Many of us have our own personal spirituality. We ponder over the most basic questions of life: *Who are we? Why are we? Where are we going?* Perhaps the elusive answers to these questions rest on a false assumption: we are trying to use logic, in a very illogical world. And possibly, we, the very finite, are groping to understand the infinite. If I had any answers they would be here, in all caps, bold-face. I will continue to experience the question-marks without the answers, though we may simply have to resort to the **LEAP OF FAITH**.

I think that Mother Teresa had a wonderful idea about faith: she did not want to convert everybody to Catholicism - she just wanted Christians to be better Christians, Muslims to be better Muslims, Jews to be better Jews, etc... Mother Teresa's view was that each of the different faiths takes its own road, but each road leads to the same God. As far as goes a blueprint showing how to get there, C.S. Lewis provides a guide-post on the last page or two of his book *Mere Christianity*.

19. EXTRA POINTS IN HEAVEN

One of my personal faith stories is about one of my greatest challenges – particularly for an Italian!

We were at Union Station in DC, some years ago, to pick up our daughter, Jennifer. Whilst waiting there, I went to the Italian eatery and bought a warm dish of baked ziti with meatballs. It was a wintry day, and when Jennifer got in the car, I decided to show her something special nearby: on the Capitol grounds, near Union Station, stands an imposing stone fountain, whose water streams different colors at night. My father, when a master stonemason, had helped build this fountain, years ago. So, we drove up, parked the car, and walked over toward the fountain, where we saw a homeless man, trying to keep warm. We started a friendly chat, when my wife said: "Why don't you open the trunk and bring the man a blanket?"

This I did. Then, she said: "Why don't you give him your baked ziti?"

My hearing is somewhat lacking, so I knew I couldn't really have heard what I thought I had heard - she couldn't have actually said that.

I was trying to think fast about how I could avoid it, but, in the end, I walked over to the car in a trance, got the baked ziti, gave it to him, and watched him eat it. I will be very upset if I didn't gain a few extra points for that in heaven!

We all have our challenges, our favorite moments and our most embarrassing moments. My favorite moments were the births of my children and granddaughter, memorizing and delivering my valedictory speech in the eighth-grade, and scoring the winning basketball shot, as time ran out, in a high-school game.

My most embarrassing moment was in high-school, but not in the classroom. I had a friend, named Harry - a good guy and a too-regular visitor at our house: Saturday mornings I would open the door and Harry would always be there. One Saturday morning, there was no Harry, and I had gone out, then came back in, saying: "Hey, Harry's not here for a change." Of course, as I said it, Harry walked out of the kitchen. I don't remember what I said after that, but it must have been pretty lame.

Years later I began thinking about

embarrassment, and decided that nobody should ever need to feel embarrassed, because whatever you've done, somebody else has done it before you. So, relax.

When you reach eighty, you are reminded daily of your own fragile mortality. You might hesitate a bit longer on the obituary page, looking at the faces of all these people you have never known; wondering about their lives and recognizing the fact that we are all a dash of water in the ocean, or a grain of sand on the beach - millions of years have passed before us, with probably many more to come. Looking at the obit photos, you realize that these people meant so much to their families and so many others; most were not celebrities and will not be widely remembered, yet I feel that their lives somehow had great significance. In this current age of international terrorism, so many lives are blotted out that we have come to expect it as a daily routine. But the wars, the killing and the violence have always been with us, and will apparently always be a part of life. One can't help but wonder why the poor are subjected to the worst violence, and why so many of us are spared.

When we were thirty, my friend used to say: "Well, we have ten more good years left." He would then say the same when we reached forty, and then fifty... he wasn't too sure after that. When you reach eighty, you are well aware that your days are growing shorter, and you try to focus on how you can best use your remaining time. I think that David Brooks would affirm that this is the time, if you haven't already done it, to work hard on your eulogy virtues, since your resumé virtues are long past.

Ta-Nehisi Coates wrote a very poignant letter to his young son, in his best-seller *Between the World and Me* - he clearly pointed out the many dangers and obstacles that a young African-American boy faces on a daily basis.

20. KEIRA, BELIEVE IN YOURSELF

I would like to include here a letter, to my only grandchild, Keira Noelle, as she celebrates her eighth birthday:

Dear Keira,

My fondest hope is that I will still be around to see you grow up, maybe even to walk down the aisle at your wedding. When I picked you up from school recently, I told you that if you ever have any questions or problems, you could ask Grandpa, and I would try to help you - you promptly replied: "When are you going to die?" Surprised by your question, I replied: "I'm not sure, but I think I'll make it to McDonald's today." (I'd planned to take Keira and a friend to McDonald's, for nuggets and a McFlurry, after school). *Keira, I hope that you will always continue to ask me questions (but, maybe easier ones).*

I remember asking you one day: "Do you know how much Grandpa loves you?" You opened your arms as wide as possible and said, enthusiastically: "This much!" I want you to remember that, whether I'm here or not, that's how much I will always love you. You were so sweet at my eightieth birthday party - you sat in my lap as I sang to you: "You're Grandpa's little girl. At the end of the rainbow, you're my pot of gold - Grandpa's little girl to have and to hold. You're sugar and spice and everything nice, and you're Grandpa's little girl." You should know how important you are to me.

I wish that I could place you in a bubble to protect you from all of the slings and arrows which confront us in life. But, we all must endure them, and there are some things that can help us along the way. I would advise you to always be kind and respectful to others; always tell the (beautiful) truth; nurture your faith; try to help others; and, most of all, believe in yourself. In my own life, I have met many naysayers, who will tell you that you can't do something - these people, and other so-called "experts", have been wrong so many times. If you know that you are right, don't listen to others - never take no for an answer. For instance, you may call some office for information, and be told that you won't get what you want; then, you might call the same office, talk to a different person and get what you want - I have experienced this, many times.

As I said, believe in yourself

*and go ahead with your
plans. Ask me and I will give
you many examples from my
life...*

Here is my prime example: years
ago, I was a press-information officer in the
federal government. Since I had previous
newspaper experience, I had some idea of
what was newsworthy - I didn't necessarily
believe that news had to be current or
recent, but that it could be something, no
matter how old, that the public didn't know.
On one occasion, I came across an item
that I considered newsworthy, wrote it and
it was approved and cleared by my local
department.   However, it had to be
approved at the departmental level, where
it was stopped, because it was not
considered newsworthy by the number one
press-chief in the department; he was also
a political appointee, with very little news
experience, and probably hoping to be
named ambassador to some country. So,
since I had my story cleared and published
in our local newsletter, I took several
copies, circled the story in red pencil and
mailed it to news outlets. The story was
published in a number of local and national

newspapers (some on the front page). I clipped these articles and sent them to the big chief of our department, hoping that I wouldn't be fired; I never heard a word back.

21. LIFE IS (STILL) UNFAIR

I have talked at length about us Geezers. Now, I must address some remarks to all of the *potential* seniors, and those youngsters who think that they will never grow old.

First, let's say that life is often (maybe *too* often) unfair. How come I'm so short and that guy is so good-looking? Why did she get the scholarship? Why didn't I get that job? That basketball coach said that I have a hawk-eye, but I would never make it at only 5'7". Our constitution guarantees freedom and equal protection, but not equal capacities or equal results.

Our life-cycle is filled with great ironies. An old proverb says: "We grow too soon old and too late smart." Unfortunately, too many critical decisions in life are made when we are least prepared. Our brains are developing gradually, when we have to react to peer-pressure, formulate sound values, choose friends, seek quality education, choose a career, maintain good physical, mental, emotional and spiritual health, select a marriage partner, raise children and try to balance family, financial and work responsibilities. Often, we go off to college with no idea of what we want to study or what career we want - many of us graduate feeling the same way. We may fall into some kind of job, and those few of us which know what they want and enjoy the work are surely blessed. I remember that basketball star Larry Bird once said that he would pay the Boston Celtics to play basketball with them - I felt that way about being a newspaper reporter; I remember thinking: *You mean that you're going to pay me for doing something I enjoy so much?*

It's very sad to think of so many who make the wrong career choice, or those who never really get a fair chance, because of poor health or some kind of addiction. These challenges can last a lifetime. My son, John, who is bright, intelligent, articulate, personable, sensitive and humorous, has had a serious drug problem for most of his life - he's been through just about every rehab program and still can't shake that demon. I will always love him, and deplore the drugs.

22. NEVER TOO OLD

He commented the other day, about so many people living longer now. I pointed out that in 1900 the average lifespan was forty-nine years - today, the average sixty-five-year-old can expect to live past eighty-three.

I am now eighty-one years of age, and I'm thinking of many people who have made valuable life contributions in their later years: how about "finger-lickin' good" Colonel Sanders, producing his Kentucky-fried chicken, or Supreme Court Justice Oliver Wendell Holmes, who wrote some of his most important opinions before he retired, at the age of ninety; baseball star Ted Williams, aged forty-two, batted 316 and hit a homerun at his last bat; Gordy Howe played professional hockey until he was fifty-two, and boxer George Foreman, forty-five, became the oldest fighter to win the world heavyweight title - he fought until he was forty-eight; critics deny that he was punch-drunk when he named all of his children "George". And, nobody ever knew exactly how old Satchel Page was when he pitched for the Cleveland Indians. These seniors had all demonstrated their share of wisdom over the years.

I think I mentioned "wisdom" before. Is there a difference between wisdom and knowledge? I might be wrong, but I think that wisdom is an inborn gift, whilst knowledge is acquired over the years. Confucius's definition of a "wise man" strikes me as accurate: he says that "a wise man is not one who knows what he knows, but one who knows what he *doesn't* know." In other words, if I take a course in basic mathematics, I could either think: *Boy, am I smart?* or: *Wow - I'll never be able to learn everything about math, because there is so much to it.*

Who are the really wise people of our time? The Dalai Lama, the Pope, C.S. Lewis, Robert Frost... many others that I'm not wise enough to remember? I love Robert Frost's little message, which he delivered on *Meet the Press*, many years ago:

"Dear God, if you forgive us for all the little jokes we play on you, we'll forgive you for the one big one that you played on us."

23. MAY WE BE REMEMBERED

This poses the question: what will you and I be remembered for?

I hope, mostly, that I will be remembered for being a good father and grandfather. If I have a tombstone, I want it inscribed only with a big question-mark, because I never knew what it was all about and, on this Earth, I never will.

I also hope that I'll be remembered for a certain apology I tried in vain to have published, a few years ago; no luck then, so I'm doing it myself, right here:

"On this national celebration day of the life of Dr. Martin Luther King, may I have the privilege of making a far-overdue, monumental apology to all of our African-American citizens, for the inexcusable, atrocious treatment of them, for far too many years. This apology is extended to our Native American brothers and sisters, to our gay community and to our Jewish brothers and sisters, for the shameful way in which they have been mistreated.

"Who am I to make such an apology? I have no official office or grand platform, from which to speak - I am only one person, but I hope that I represent thousands, hopefully millions, who feel as I do. So, with all due respect, we ask that somehow you will accept our most sincere apology and realize that there are so many of us who deeply regret our past mistakes."

We all hope to be remembered.
What will you be remembered for?

ABOUT THE AUTHOR

Born in Washington, DC, Tony Anastasi graduated from Gonzaga High School and the University of Maryland, at College Park. He was a sports writer for the *Washington Daily News* and, in the early sixties, joined the federal government as a public information officer. Now retired, he lives in Rockville, MD, where he still pulls pranks on his wife, Jeanne.

ABOUT THE PUBLISHER

L.R. Price Publications is dedicated to publishing books by unknown authors.
We use a mixture of both traditional and modern publishing options to bring our authors' words to the wider world.

We print, publish, distribute and market books in a variety of formats including paper and hard back, e-books, digital audio books and online.

If you're, an author interested in getting your book published; or a book retailer interested in selling our books, please contact us.

www.lrpricepublications.com
L.R. Price Publications Ltd,
27 Old Gloucester Street,
London, WC1N 3AX.
(0203) 0519572
publishing@lrprice.com

Anthony J. Anastasi

www.ingramcontent.com/pod-product-compliance
Lightning Source LLC
Chambersburg PA
CBHW060127050426
42448CB00010B/2032